A LOVERS JOURNEY

A LOVERS JOURNEY

NAKEISA JACKSON

Copyright © 2020 by Nakeisa Jackson All rights reserved Published by beyondthebookmedia.com

All rights reserved. No part of this publication may be reproduced, distributed, or transmitted in any form or by any means, including photocopying, recording, or other electronic or mechanical methods, without the prior written permission of the publisher, except in the case of brief quotations embodied in critical reviews and certain other noncommercial uses permitted by copyright law. For permission requests, write to the publisher, addressed "Attention: Permissions Coordinator," at the address below.

Limit of Liability/Disclaimer of Warranty: While the publisher and author have used their best efforts in preparing this book, they make no representations of warranties with respect to the accuracy or completeness of the contents of this book and specifically disclaim any implied warranties or merchantability or fitness for a particular purpose. No warranty may be created or extended by sales representatives or written sales materials. The advice and strategies contained herein may not be suitable for your situation. You should consult with a professional where appropriate. Neither the publisher nor author shall be liable for damages arising here from.

Beyond The Book Media, LLC
Alpharetta, GA

www.beyondthebookmedia.com

The publisher is not responsible for websites that are not owned by the publisher.

ISBN - 978-1-953788-10-8

I dedicate this book to my first true love God. Might sound cliché, but He absolutely is and if it wasn't for his saving grace I wouldn't be here. I also dedicate this to the reader of this book; I believe God led you here for a reason and I pray you get something out of it.

TABLE OF CONTENTS

Chapter I
Love Introduced.. 9

Chapter II
What is Love Anyway?.. 21

Chapter III
Loving God's Way.. 31

Chapter IV
How Loving Myself Looked in my life................................... 44

Chapter V
How Loving Myself Looked in my life................................... 55

Chapter VI
Loving into Purpose.. 65

References.. 78

CHAPTER I
LOVE INTRODUCED

Love is patient, love is kind, it does not envy, it does not boast. This is something that I heard from the time I knew about the bible. It's probably second to the Adam and Eve creation story. The creation story I could digest but love I couldn't. Although I heard this story, I never knew what it really meant in my life. The examples that set love up for me didn't look like the definition we find in 1 Corinthians 13. I really didn't know what love was. I thought it was a feeling that came with heartache and disappointment.

As a child, I had a vivid imagination. I had wild dreams and spent a lot of time daydreaming. One of the most memorable daydreams I had was about my future relationship. To my knowledge, most little girls think about their future wedding and how beautiful the dress will be. That wasn't the story I formulated. The story I imagined was of a man that I loved repaying me by treating me wrong; and then making up with me in order to make me feel better. I created the concept that love was supposed to hurt in some form. I imagined it was supposed to be this whole 'break up to make-up' situation. I got this idea from my parents and home environment. My father and mother divorced when I was very young, so I had a stepmother from the time my mother left my father. I watched my father and stepmother have their share of breakups and makeups, and I watched my mother, in her various relationships, do the same. As a young girl they were my examples, so I felt like that was what love must be. I began to believe I couldn't be loved unless we had been through some things and went through cycles of loving each other then hurting each other. This thought process stuck with me through most of life along with many other false concepts of love.

My childhood also taught me that love was a feeling. I had to feel love for it to be real. I gained this perception from the death of loved ones at a very young age. One evening after school, we were preparing for bed, when my mother got a phone call. I could sense the panic in the conversation. Once she got off the phone, she rushed in and told me to quickly get dressed. We got into the car and rushed down the highway. A few moments later we arrived at my grandparents' house. We all got out of the car and a lot of my family was there. That is when the news was broken to me that my grandmother passed away. I knew that she was sick but did not really understand at 8 years old. At the news of her death, everyone was crying. I looked around, trying to figure out why? I thought they must love her, and I don't. I thought I loved her, but since there was no tears, I had to be doing it wrong. I didn't feel anything. The death of my grandmother made me questioned what love really was for the first time. I felt that I should have maybe loved her, but how can you feel love for your family when, at eight, love was only possible in relationships with people you wanted to be your partner?

As I grew older, I began to have an overwhelming sense that I would never be good enough to experience love that didn't hurt. Love was supposed to only come from other people.

I knew my mother loved me because she yelled and whopped me. I knew my uncles loved me because they threatened me a lot about dealing with boys. I had no leverage to love them back. Honestly, my family would easily be a casualty of war. They told me they loved me, and this was what it looked like, but I didn't like the way love looked or felt. I became rebellious in a sense. I did what I wanted to do. They said these things made me better but when I did better, it still hurt. Therefore, love was not something I wanted anything to do with. It left me with more confusion.

I began to create my own definition of what love should be. I thought as long as you didn't hurt my feelings, I could accept the love you gave me. As long as you didn't do that, I could show you a form of love that didn't require us to be in a romantic relationship. I really felt that love isn't supposed to hurt when it came outside of family. If you hurt me that meant you weren't family and, therefore, you got no love. During this time, as you may can see, I never knew that it was possible, or even acceptable to love myself. I also didn't realize that loving myself was the key to loving others and so many other things in life. Without knowing these things, I definitely didn't understand that God could love someone like me.

The second is this: 'Love your neighbor as yourself.' [a] There is no commandment greater than these."- Mark 12:31. NIV

As I entered young adulthood, I began to have relationships with men. My first encounter with a man happened at 17. He was 21 years old, and he was in a relationship with a baby on the way. I met him at a train station. I thought he was so attractive, and I was in love at first sight. It didn't matter what came out of his mouth; he was interested in me. Growing up, I was always bigger than the other kids. No one my age wanted to be seen with me. They liked me but would never admit it publicly in school. I thought this was love because, to be honest, it didn't hurt my feelings. I was accustomed to being hidden, being last, not good enough. This actually affirmed what I thought about myself. Hence why this twenty-one-year-old man being interested in me was right up, my ally. I was too young, but he liked me, so it made me rationalize why we couldn't be seen together much.

While dealing with him, I literally would have to watch him walk past me, get far enough away then go to his house. The mother of his baby was out of town, but no one could see us together because that would mess up his flow. He promised me that he really wanted me. He hadn't hurt my feelings, and he made me feel what I thought love was. We were having lots of sex, and he said things that made me feel good about myself during that time. I was really "in love" with him; sprung. This love I had made me do things I deem crazy now, including going to his house and just walking right in looking for him. He wasn't home; I didn't call or anything, I just went. I thank God he protected me because that could have been bad. Eventually, this relationship ended, and it hurt so badly. But it didn't stop my bad decisions in relationships. I just replaced him with someone else

By this age, sex equaled love. It felt good to me, so if you wanted to have sex with me, you loved me. This concept had me feeling love and disappointment a lot. When I couldn't get it from one person, I tried the next and the next until one wouldn't hurt me. It continued. I continued to be hurt. These relationships created another concept in my head that I learned long ago, love is supposed to hurt because everyone I loved, that I thought loved me as well, hurt me. This made me believe that everyone loved the same. I thought all men and women were the same. I knew I didn't like it, so I didn't know what I was doing wrong.

"If the world hates you, know that it has hated me before it hated you. If you were of the world, the world would love you as its own; but because you are not of the world, but I chose you out of the world; therefore the world hates you John 15:18-19. ESV

I was someone who would fight for you to like me or choose me over everyone else. Risk something for me so I could know you love me. I remember enjoying the fact that in school, some boys would ignore me, but at home, they would be all in my face. I thought they really loved me; however, I grew up and learned that this, in fact, couldn't possibly be love. It had to be the complete opposite. I started to believe that love was a joke, and that I loved differently.

I had seen love in the movies, and I loved like Cinderella loved Prince Charming. I wanted my happily ever after no matter what it came with, so I began to attract controlling men. These men would sometimes cheat, but we would make up. It matched my daydream, and we would be in love all over again. I knew they loved me because they didn't leave me. In fact, they fought me if I tried to leave. I had finally found the perfect combo to love. Every man was this way, so I knew this was love. I thought the key was titling the relationship because these men didn't care that I was bigger. I looked good as a nineteen-year-old on a twenty-nine-year-old man's arm. They knew what to say, how to say it, and they took care of me. The other concept of love I had was you take care of what you love. If you made me feel good, paid my bills and controlled me, or was very jealous; you loved me. This was the only type of loving I was worthy of.

For God so loved the world, that he gave his only Son, that whoever believes in him should not perish but have eternal life. John 3:16. ESV

During this time of confusion and looking for love, there were two significant romantic relationships that would change my life forever. One of those relationships led me to Christ but also changed my life in ways I could never imagine. I would say these two relationships led me into the fullness of what God's love is. I gave my life to Christ, or should I say religion at 18. I remember the day like it was yesterday. I was arguing with my boyfriend who was 26 years old. I told him, I wanted to go to church and he was completely against the idea. Due to all the arguing and fighting, it pushed me towards church. I knew he wouldn't come.

I came into the church that cold January morning just to listen to service and run away from the horrific relationship I was in. The whole service, I felt a sense of peace that overwhelmed me. I don't remember the sermon, but I remember when the church doors opened. I walked to the altar call and gave my life to Christ. It was a feeling I can't even describe. One thing I was happy to learn about was the saving grace of God. I was excited about this new life I would receive as a result of one decision. One month later I was baptized. I read the bible, went to church, and learn what I shouldn't be doing. I learned how I would go to heaven second class if I didn't stay away from sin. All I knew about God was that he was a harsh God who hated sinners, and I didn't want to be hated. I learned this concept following the rules and stipulations of religion. No one was talking about God's love or loving yourself. They only said we should love our neighbor, oh, and Jesus. How do you do that? I was adamant that I would do whatever it took to make God happy.

A few months after being saved, I received some of the most devastating news, that no one would ever want to receive. I got a phone call about test results. I learned that I was HIV positive. After I received this diagnosis, I cried for months. How could God save me to kill me? Based off what I was taught, he was so good if you did what he said. Why didn't he stop this? I literally got saved and never went back to the guy who I believe infected me. I immediately began to feel entitled and bargained with God. I even told God that nothing bad should ever happen to me ever again. I was doing everything he requested of me so therefore, I should always be in his good graces. It didn't take long for me to realize; this is simply unrealistic in my walk as a believer. Although this was true, there were so many great things that were in store for me.

After the end of this first relationship, I had a very negative view of myself. This diagnosis made me feel less than and unworthy of anything good. Soon after I met another man. He was 10 years older than I was. I just knew he would love all my broken areas because who would do a girl living with HIV wrong? One thing I learned in that relationship, is that my brokenness was showing, and some people don't mind taking advantage of that.

When we first met, the relationship seemed like a typical relationship he said and did all the right things. Before long we lived together. I still was totally in love with God and wanting to do right. I struggled in this area with men, severely. Although we lived together, I tried abstinence, stayed active in church and in the bible. This would come to an extreme halt when the cheating started. Due to my low self-esteem I thought I needed to do whatever was necessary to keep him happy. I chose him over God. I loved him and I thought he loved me. It was important that I showed him through sexual contact. Soon after, I realized he was still the same person. He still cheated on me and even started to be abusive to me. We would physically fight all the time. It started to wear me out in ways I couldn't imagine. It was obvious, from being in this relationship I didn't even really know what love was to me at that time in life. I just knew I loved differently. This relationship was the one that made me cry out to God. I was tired of being run over and used, so I stepped away from church and relationships for a while. I wanted to learn myself. I would say this was the Holy Spirit. I found the courage and strength to end this five-year relationship that took a toll on me. I was leaving teenage hood when we met, and now I was in early adulthood. I had grown up a lot and knew I was different, and I felt an unction to get closer to God. I didn't know why because, honestly, I thought God hated me. Based on what I learned from church, I was just the type that God despised.

1 Corinthians 6:19-20 Do you not know that your bodies are temples of the Holy Spirit, who is in you, whom you have received from God? You are not your own; 20 you were bought at a price. Therefore, honor God with your bodies. NIV. 1 Corinthians 6:19-20.

When this relationship ended, I had just graduated from college with a nursing degree. I had my freedom back and wanted to get to know God better. My view of God was still so skewed, I didn't know how to go about it. When you don't go further to seek God, intentionally you open yourself back into opportunities to keep doing what you always knew. Being alone brought back those same things that were there before this relationship, I spent so much time in. I had bad thoughts about myself. Still, I still felt unworthy of anything good and believed love only came when something bad was attached to it. This time I experienced depression more so than anything. It wasn't only the weight they had to be ok with, but my diagnosis was also attached to it.

I didn't want to be like the man who gave this to me, I couldn't just tell people. So, it depressed me. I was learning my dislikes in men so I could choose the opposite because, again, I'm in a position where they had to pick me, and I couldn't pick them. That stung, to be honest. I seriously had loved all wrong in my head, and God slowly but surely began to show me that I continued to walk with God, he used my love of relationships and validation of men to teach me how to love myself, how to love Him, and how to receive true genuine love from others.

Love is patient, love is kind. It does not envy, it does not boast, it is not proud. It does not dishonor others, it is not self-seeking, it is not easily angered, it keeps no record of wrongs. Love does not delight in evil but rejoices with the truth. It always protects, always trusts, always hopes, always perseveres. Love never fails." ~ 1 Corinthians 13:4-8. NIV

Those words that sat in 1 Corinthians weren't just words. They meant something. This was God's description of love. As a baby in Christ, I didn't quite understand how different the world was from God. I knew the world was full of sin, and God was sinless, but I didn't understand that He is the total opposite of the world. From my experiences, your life was always about someone else. It was never about you. Loving me, the way God loves me, was a concept that was far away from reality.

Once I began to get deliverance from different things like having low self-esteem, perfectionism, and people-pleasing, I broke through with Love for myself. I began to really learn what I like and didn't like. I started to watch what I said to myself. I started to be intentional about my time with God and learn me. I started to understand why "Christians" said all these statements that I thought were just words. This love started overflowing into everything around me. I stopped with the negative self-talk and I stopped gossiping about everyone and everything. I prayed, forgave people, and showed grace. This only happened as a result of learning God's love and loving me.

As I grew in God's love, I was by myself. I was in a rough season of marriage; I had just miscarried two times and nothing mattered to me at that time except God. I didn't know a lot, but I knew that He helped me get through the negative feelings around HIV, so he could get me through this. Plus, I felt like He owed me an explanation for everything that was happening to me. I soon learned my faults and how the enemy was plotting and trying to paralyze me in my life.

When you are in a season where it's just you and God, you only can look at you; the woman or man in the mirror. You can only correct yourself because there is no one else there to correct. I felt like I was walking around with a mirror in my face. I no longer had a mask. I had to look at every blemish on my face, every curve on my body, and every strain of my hair. I had to learn how to love all of me at any state, at any place. Before, I began to build my relationship with God I spent the majority of my life trying to change me; I tried changing my weight, my hair, and how I dealt with people. I did all of these things and in the end it wasn't sustainable. I spent a lot of time going backwards, in this season I moved differently.

In this particular season, I had to move forward. I refused to be bound. I had really gotten saved. I attended a new church, and I got delivered at the first service I attended. I began to drop my bad addictive habits, and I set boundaries in my life. I could no longer just let things happen to me. I had to learn my triggers so I could move in the realm God created me to be in.

For I know the plans I have for you," declares the LORD, "plans to prosper you and not to harm you, plans to give you hope and a future. Jeremiah 29:11 NIV

I had this renewed energy to chase after God and the love he talked about. I wanted to know what it was like to love me. It was a weird concept, but I heard that it worked. I listened to the world and their track record was poor. I had to follow what God was saying because his track record had been great. I had learned to trust him, and I knew he wouldn't lead me astray. I thought learning love and chasing after the heart of God would be worth it.

Guess what? It was worth it. By operating in obedience, I learned how to love myself into purpose. Into the real purpose that God has in my life. Little did I know that my purpose was tied directly into teaching people about love, healing after miscarriages, deliverance, breakthrough, and marriage. Learning that this was indeed one of the many purposes, God created me for, didn't fully hit me until I wrote this book.

Over a year ago, I created a love challenge, and I sat on it for over a year because I didn't know what to do with it. In my opinion it was created before time, however, had I continued pressing into God in that season I backslid, I would have seen that it was actually right on time. I led myself into a waiting season because I left God and the purpose He placed in me. I didn't want to help women with the issues deeper than the diagnosis of being HIV positive. I thought I met my marks when, in actuality, my HIV diagnosis would be the vessel that led me to this place of writing devotional style books and teaching others how to dig deeper with God.

Do everything in love. 1 Corinthians 16:14 NIV

God has called us to love in all things we do, and loving His people is a top priority. You, yes you, are one of His people. We only can love our neighbors as much as we love ourselves. Loving yourself can free you to move and be bold about God in purpose. You will no longer suffer from being timid, embarrassed, and ashamed. It will allow you to move more effectively when you do the work of the Lord. We have to handle the kingdom with care. We are all one body.

Just as a body, though one, has many parts, but all its many parts form one body, so it is with Christ. 13 For we were all baptized by[c] one Spirit so as to form one body—whether Jews or Gentiles, slave or free—and we were all given the one Spirit to drink. 14 Even so, the body is not made up of one part but of many. 1 Corinthians 12:12-14. NIV

When you care for your body, you don't just take care of one piece of you, you take care of the whole body. This is how I now look at the ministry overall. I believe we all have a role to play in the body and it starts with one of the fruits of the spirit, love. God is love, and we too can be love. I share my journey of love with you, because I do believe that loving yourself and others is one of the primary keys to learning your purpose. Whether you know your purpose or not without love, you won't be able to walk into it, in the way God chose you to do it.

CHAPTER II
WHAT IS LOVE ANYWAY?

I remember the first time my mother told me she loved me. I was 12. She went on to say it again twice in one day when I graduated from college. Up to this point, I never heard the words from the mouth of my mother. I just had to depend on her actions to determine her love for me. As I began this journey of self-love, I really wanted to know what love was apart from what I saw growing up. All I knew was the bad examples I grew up with and that as a teenager, I had not lived long enough to understand love at all. The feelings I had for men weren't love, at least that's what I was being told. If that isn't love, then what is it. Because that love felt good to me, even though I was doing the one thing that I had been told I should be saving for marriage.

But God demonstrates his own love for us in this: While we were still sinners, Christ died for us. Romans 5:8. NIV

I want to take you on a dive about what definitions of love actually exist and demonstrate how that affected my life in various ways. According to Dictionary.com, love is an intense feeling of deep affection, a great interest, or pleasure in something. This definition of love definitely aligned with what I thought love was without the hurting part. I felt this intense feeling for the men I had sex with.

I also had great interest and pleasure in many hobbies. I was very interested in some of my friends and even during a season in my life, lovers of the same sex. Per this definition, I knew what love was.

Another definition of love is strong affection for another arising out of kinship or personal ties. This would cover the love that came from my family. It's a strong affection that arises out of being related to one another. As I really began to research this, I had to conclude that there is more than one type of love. The type of love we should all strive for is the definition that God set for us. This love is known as agape. Agape is the type of love that God has for all of his children. It means to love without condition, and I learned how to love in this manner, after getting married and going through more difficult seasons.

Jesus told him, You must love the Lord your God with all your heart, with all your soul, and with all your mind. This is the greatest and most important commandment. Matthew 22:37-38. ISV

At the time that I got married, I choose my husband for several reasons; but one of the major ones was that he really loved me. He didn't mind showing me affection in public. If a man thought I looked good, it made him appreciate me anymore. He gave me so much confidence. I thought his thoughts matched mine about me. I loved him the same way he showed me love. I complimented him a lot and made it known he was mine. I acted crazy and all but there were some areas we both failed in. My husband broke the golden rule. Do not hurt my feelings, ever. He did it, and I checked out. I vowed I would never divorce, so I had to sit in it. Every time I considered it, God came to me and said, that's not my will. I want you to love him. How in the world could I love a man that caused so much pain?

8 Whoever does not love does not know God, because God is love. 9 This is how God showed his love among us: He sent his one and only Son into the world that we might live through him. 10 This is love: not that we loved God, but that he loved us and sent his Son as an atoning sacrifice for our sins. 1 John 4:8-10. NIV

God sent me a group of angels that started talking about the various types of loves that existed. This is where I got the throat punch; the type of love I needed to learn was the one that has the potential to hurt me the most. Agape love is loving with no condition. No matter what happened between you and someone, you still loved them. The first thought of the concept made me upset, to be honest. That sounded like a pushover, especially as it related to my marriage.

Traditionally, I loved people how they loved me and hurt people how they hurt me. So, the concept of loving like this didn't work out well in my mind. I stayed married, but I spent a long time being on a hamster wheel because I wanted to love my way. At this point, I knew that the type of things my husband was doing gave me an out, although God said that's not what he wanted. I wanted to feel loved, though, and I didn't feel it. So, I fed l into many things that made me feel love.

To fully show more of how I got this concept I want to take you back into my life as a teenager and before my HIV diagnosis. As a teenager, my first experiences of feeling love came through contact with other girls. I had girlfriends all over the place and girls who I touched before. Honestly, I began to have encounters with girls, either touching inappropriately or suggesting it to other girls after I was introduced to it in elementary school. I thought that girls were beautiful and since boys didn't like me, I decided to explore with girls. I remember being in fourth grade, touching on a girl in the back of the classrooms in daycare. I also had girls outside of schools that I played house with. It brought me pleasure, or what I eventually thought was love. Then, after being heartbroken, I went on to deal with boys and men who made me feel the same.

My first real boyfriend, who I liked seriously, I met in the 12th grade. I was about 17 ½. I thought he was the best thing that happened to me. He loved me or so he said and was the first person who I exclusively had sex with. He met my family; he would come to my house all the time and my family adored him. Honestly, I think they were happy he wasn't a girl. Although this attraction for women had not left yet. I was in my own world with this boy, until he cheated on me just like the women did. He took it to the extreme and even got a few women pregnant, I thank God, I wasn't one of them. This was the straw that broke the camel's back. It opened a raw area of brokenness that led me on a path to destruction.

After being heartbroken for the second time, I would not put up with anybody doing me wrong especially not a person of the opposite sex. At this time in my life, due to being so broken, I started to give my partners whatever they dished out and then some. If you made me mad or wouldn't do what I asked you to, I would cheat on you or leave you. I couldn't hold down a relationship longer than 3 months. Since, I couldn't seem to stay in relationships long, I grew jealous of people in long-term relationships. I turned into someone I didn't recognize. I started to have multiple boyfriends and sex partners. I was so tired of being hurt and disappointed, I thought why not play the game with them.

After the end of this relationship, I had a lot of encounters with men, but once I made it to college, I decided I wanted something different. I was tired of it all and decided, just maybe I should be alone. After dating from the age of 15-18, I knew it had to be something better. I knew there had to be a reason, people were in long term relationships and I wasn't. During my first semester of college is when I met the man who I contracted HIV from. He was one of the few men I allowed to have sex with me without a condom, although it didn't start that way. I truly thought he seriously loved me. I was very serious about our relationship although it too was short. Soon he showed me that, he didn't love me he just was a predator. He was actually preying on me. The emotions of being HIV positive, made me feel like I lost my value and my self-esteem plummeted.

During this time, if you knew me you would never be able to tell how low I was. I kept a smile on my face, and I partied hard. I was living in secret wanting somebody, anybody to just love me. Six months after my diagnosis, I found a man who was willing to accept my status and it ended up being a five-year relationship that lasted five years too long. This is the same relationship I mentioned in the previous chapter, but I need you to really understand what this relationship taught me.

I met him on a bus, and he sold me a dream. He told me he lived with his cousin, he had his own car and a good job. He even made up a story about why he was on a bus that day. Within a week of meeting him, he took me to school and really tried to be this "person" he claimed to be. I thought, I had found me a real man. He was 10 years older than me so for him to have this so-called life, he claimed made sense. After about a month, I told him my status was fine with it, but he wasn't comfortable with it. For him, I was good enough to be with him, have sex with him be like a wife to him, but I never could talk about it and the desires God put in my heart to do with this diagnosis. He was adamant that I never tell people either because then it may be thought that he too had it. It was a controlling relationship, to be honest, but I was used to that. I actually thought it meant he loved me. The previous relationships I was in had some element of control to them, which added to my illusion of what love really was.

At this point, I still had lingering my "what I learned from childhood about love" on me. It didn't matter how bad the relationship was; I was determined. I also was given a promise of marriage to him. He told me after I graduated, we would get married. It didn't matter that we fought, he cheated and threaten my life on multiple occasions. He loved me and said it often, so nothing else really mattered because this was love as I knew it. During this season, I thought the longer the time, the more you loved him. Really, I had gotten trapped in a cycle.

There are a few things I now reflect on when I think about that relationship. One thing that kept me bound was his unbelief in God. I remember wanting to be abstinent and telling him I am doing it. He initially said ok, cool but in actuality, he wasn't cool with it. I found out he just did what was necessary to make sure he got the sex he desired. I was not aware the majority of the relationship because I had two jobs and school to focus on. When I discovered the cheating is when, I would start back having sex with him. I thought he went and sought love from someone else because I wasn't loving him.

Another thing that sticks out as a representation of love were the fights. When we met, he would tell me how he fought his ex. He actually bragged on some horrible things he had done. I thought I was exempt from any of these things happening to me. I just knew I was stronger than she was, and I would never be like her. I was very young and felt like I was the apple of his eye, and he wouldn't dare touch me. I was wrong. The violence I experienced included humiliating things, including him throwing things out the window while in the car, accusing me of cheating in public places, and destroying property in our apartment. Some situations that occurred are hard to remember at this time, it was a very traumatizing time for me. During this period, it was hard to recognize the abuse as it was mental and emotional abuse.

He spent a lot of time accusing me of cheating, manipulating me, and putting me in hard situations. One thing he did that made me feel I had to prove my love to him was retaliation. If I went out somewhere with anybody, he had to do the same thing. One day I went out to celebrate a birthday at a club. Since I was going out, he also went out. He chose to go to a club in the same area. During this time, I drank a lot of alcohol. I was a stressed student, very close to becoming a nurse. When the club I was at was over, he told me to go to our car and wait for him to leave the club where he was. I was drunk, so normally out of fear I would have waited. However, this time I had a family member there with me, who took me home. He came home four hours later, and I was in a drunken stupor. All of a sudden, I felt punches to my stomach. He was screaming and yelling, asking me who took me home. All I could do was ball up and cry.

After that incident, I knew that I had to leave. I spent a lot of time asking God to take me out of the situation. During this time, I couldn't see past where I was, and I wanted God to use his magical powers to come and save me. I felt like it wasn't happening. I made all these deadlines to leave, and I just couldn't. I really believed that if I left, I would never be loved again. No one would understand me or my diagnosis. Eventually, I got out of the situation. It took for me to just grow up. I literally couldn't handle the relationship anymore; it was changing me into someone else.

At the time, I didn't realize how messed up this form of love had me; I was confused, lost, and far away from God. As I found the strength to leave, I again wanted to be closer to God. I realized was actually God calling me to learn more about Himself and love. When I left the relationship, I would scream from the mountain top how free I felt, but behind closed doors, depression was very real. I didn't even know that's what it was at the time.

The winter after the end of the relationship, I was very lonely and living alone. I had nice material things, an apartment, a car, and a career. I was very young too, so I could do anything I wanted after I paid my bills. However, there was something missing, and I was sad. I spent a lot of time working and the rest of the time sleeping. I would miss whole days and get a lot of voicemails from family saying how they will send someone for me if I didn't call them. I always had a good excuse that they believed because I worked at night. I remember several days of coming home from work, and the enemy would tell me to just run my car into the median. He would tell me it would all be over then. I really thought I was crazy and just depressed and pitiful. These were the words I said about myself. I can't even fix my mouth to speak that now.

I have said these things to you, that in me you may have peace. In the world, you will have tribulation. But take heart; I have overcome the world. John 16:33 NIV

I was so thankful that I didn't take myself out. After about six months of changes, turmoil, and me continuing to dip back into my security blanket, my ex, I finally began to choose me. I wasn't out the clear, but things were getting clearer as far as my necessity to learn about God; the one who placed me here to live this life. I needed to know why and what He wanted from me. I knew that I had a strong gift that I couldn't place a name on and was afraid of, and I knew He told me to become a nurse. I owed it to myself to go and get that.

As soon as I decided to give up on men, I met the man who would eventually become my husband. I wish I could tell you I was whole when I met him, but I was a whole mess. I became a woman I didn't recognize and went deeper into mess. That mess was something I turned into a whole message.

Due to all the craziness I had been through with loving in the wrong way, when I met my husband, I wanted to be a new girl. I wanted to be the girl with confidence, who did what she wanted and didn't care anything about love. I wanted God, though. See? Clearly, I didn't understand the concept of God in this season. How could I want God and not understand love? Love was his greatest command. I didn't understand it, at least not in His way. I desired to be ratchet because I was the nice homey girl that was better as a friend. I was done with her, I turned into the complete opposite.

In the beginning of our relationship as boyfriend and girlfriend, we were both afraid of new relationships, so we just enjoyed each other with no label. He loved me a lot, and I could tell. It drew me closer to him, I was crazy about him and in the beginning, I showed it. I remember one day I said I wasn't about to keep showing him all these love signals because I needed to be prepared for when he hurt me. I backed off some. In my backing off, I started to do things that made me feel like I had one up on him. I continued to talk to other men via phone; never sexually. I would tell him it wasn't a big deal, so he shouldn't be concerned. That was me in protection mode. The things my last boyfriend showed me as love, I showed him. I started to be sneaky and deceitful and justified it because sex wasn't involved. I never thought about his emotions or feelings, just my own.

In a sense, because someone had showed me how to give love the wrong way, when someone was trying to give me the type of love I deserved, I couldn't receive it. I pushed it all away, almost to the point of no return. Within the first few months of us being official we broke up, I started to have inappropriate conversations with exes and people that I had some type of interest in, therefore he retaliated. He began to hurt me back in a revengeful manner, so we broke up and didn't reconnect until we were engaged. In my first book, I talked about how we were separate for nine months because we both had work to do. Did we get it all during the nine months? No, but we are getting it now. As I was forced to press into God after marriage, I began to learn about real love; God's love. The type of love that covered a multitude of sin, the love that you could do nothing to get, and nothing could take it away. Real Agape love. It was something I never knew existed.

CHAPTER III
LOVING GOD'S WAY

We have heard the scripture over and over again about what love is because the bible has a detailed definition. One thing I realized as I looked into the main scripture that defines God's love, is love is a noun because all the words describe love. I also realize that love isn't an emotion at all. Get that. Love from GOD is a feeling. It's something that has a lot of actions that bring about other fruits of the spirit.

But the fruit of the Spirit is love, joy, peace, forbearance, kindness, goodness, faithfulness, gentleness, and self-control. Against such things, there is no law. Galatians 5:22-23. NIV

His love is meant to change you and give you things you won't find anywhere else unless you have God in your life. I think it's very important that we understand every part of this love scripture to really understand how God needs you to treat and love people. As we previously discussed, there are several types of love, but only one like God. As you study your bible, it's important that you learn that God addressed things that were against the world's understanding. So, He didn't put those words there because He just like to tell us what to do. He wants us to understand what love really is. I believe this is also why He sent Jesus down to show us what this looks like. That way, when Jesus went back to the kingdom and left us with the Holy Spirit, we could know and give that type of love to ourselves and others.

4 Love is patient, love is kind. It does not envy, it does not boast, it is not proud. 5 It does not dishonor others, it is not self-seeking, it is not easily angered, it keeps no record of wrongs. 6 Love does not delight in evil but rejoices with the truth. 7 It always protects, always trusts, always hopes, always perseveres. 1 Corinthians 13:4-7. NIV

The first thing He shares is that love is patient. According to Google (2020), patience means to have the capacity to tolerate delay, trouble, or suffering without getting upset or angry[a]. Now, that's in the world. Biblically, we must add willingness. Patience is to have the willingness to tolerate these delays without losing it. We are required to be willing to wait on the Lord to do what He said He would do. The difference I see is that in the world, we may say we have patience, but we get mad, cry, kick, and scream the whole way. We do not actually do it without losing it. When looking at the example of patience in the world, it can apply to many things, including the things we have no choice except to wait for. For example, when we are pregnant, the baby is coming in nine months. No matter how fast we want it to be over to meet our baby, we have to wait.

Patience in God's way has a lot to do with choice. Being patient in the way God would like us to be, we don't have to wait. We can manipulate a situation or rush into if we choose to. God wants us to be willing to wait on him and his timing for every aspect of our lives. I know right now Holy Spirit is reminding you of something that God needs you to be willing to be patient for. He wants us to be patient and do it with grace; just as He has been with us. Think about how God is patient with us. We spent years choosing someone else over God, and when you were ready, He still opened His loving arms and took you in. It doesn't matter what you have done and how long it takes, He is there for you.

Love is kind. Did you realize there is a difference between kindness and niceness? Think about it. Sometimes in error, we use the words interchangeably. They don't mean the same thing. To be nice is to be agreeable. An example is when you see something that you know is wrong. You can choose to correct the person in love or just be agreeable although you know that you know that's not the right thing, but the easy thing to do. In kindness, correction is a part of that. According to the Merriam-Webster dictionary, to be kind is to be of a forbearing nature or being of a sympathetic nature[b] (2020). Then, kindness is the quality of being kind. It's to be of a nature that isn't necessarily agreeing but forgiving. So, I might not like what you are doing but I'm not going to go off on you about it. Biblically, kindness means that you show mercy and grace when you don't have to or when there may not be a reward for you on the other end. So, God shows us kindness even when we can't give anything back. We are so undeserving, but He does it anyway. So, you may fall back into an old habit and God gives you grace. The thing about His kindness is He will convict your heart, but He does it with so much love. This kindness can be hard for us as humans. Think about this, how many of you would send your only son to save a world that hated you. That's what God did for us. Even though He would live again, He still had to go through things we never will have to go through. Think about how much Jesus loves us too. I don't know if God asked me to come back here to help a whole bunch of people who hated him, if I would have been that willing. God also shows his kindness by helping us when we put ourselves in certain situations. It's also important to realize that God uses kindness to lead us to repentance[c]. When loving people, this is what God wants us to do.

It does not envy, it does not boast, it is not proud. 1 Corinthians 4 NIV

After He tells us two things that love is, He lets us know three things it is not. It is not envious; it doesn't boast and it's not proud. So, let's start with envy. In this season, I have learned that love is not jealous. As I was growing up, I was very envious. I was the friend that didn't want you to be friends with anyone else. I was so jealous. If a girl was smaller than me, or got more attention from boys or the teachers, it was a problem. I didn't get a lot of attention at home, so I depended on other sources to give me attention. I was the oldest child on my mother side and in the middle on my father side. These two positions sometimes leave you left out. I had a very envious spirit connected to me. I believe this was passed down to me in my lineage. Now that I understand discerning spirits, I see it a lot in my family and in the world. I know that this is a spirit because I am genuinely happy for people and I'll get on Facebook and look at someone's accomplishments and then thoughts of jealousy try to come to me. Now that I am aware, I start to dive deep to see whether it's something that I need to work on or the enemy's camp dropping seeds of jealousy. It didn't take long to realize that it wasn't me and I had to cut it at the root. Dealing with envy can lead to comparison and bitterness that will derail your journey to purpose. If these things are coming up, it's important that you take it to God.

One of my purposes in life is the ability to connect people and to pour into people who lead. If a jealous spirit attaches to me, then I literally wouldn't be able to get over myself and reach out to people, who I am called to serve by God. I think it was important God listed out what it didn't do so we could recognize when we are not operating in love.

The second thing about love is it doesn't boast. To boast essentially means to brag. According to the Merriam dictionary, boast means to praise oneself extravagantly in speech: speak of oneself with excessive pride[d]. That hit hard, so to show off or have excessive pride in oneself is not operating in love. I want to be clear that it didn't say you can't be proud of yourself or talk about your accomplishments. The key word is excessive. When you perform acts or have accomplished something, you do not have to go around and talk about your accomplishments to the point of boasting. When we look at boasting biblically, it can be good when properly applied. When we talk about how great God is, that type of boasting is great. When operating in love, it simply isn't apart from how love works. So, when you love unconditionally it's not your place to mention what you did for someone. You do it willingly. I will say that I have been guilty of boasting and sharing all the things I have done for people who were unable to return the favor. I know now that I did that because of pride and operating out of the will of God.

The third thing about love is that it is not proud. We have so much pride to the point that sometimes we don't even realize that we have pride issues. Pride is a feeling or deep pleasure or satisfaction derived from one's own achievements, the achievements of those with whom one is closely associated, or from qualities or possessions that are widely admired[e]. Pride, according to the world, is all about having deep pleasure in your own success. So, it doesn't mean you always express it as in boasting but it's directed towards you. When we look at it in biblical terms it means that you prefer your own will over God's will. I thought this was deep, because I think about all the times when God called me to do something that I refused to do because of pride. When we use this in the operation of love, we fail at loving God's way. I thank God He isn't prideful with us when He loves us. I can only imagine if God decided to be prideful; we would probably all would just perish.

Last year I came up with this great idea on how I can make money in my business by helping people write. Although I knew

God had called me to do something different, I didn't see the fruit of it as fast as I wanted, so I made the decision to pivot. Originally, God called me to write books and create content. But, when I wrote my first book, I didn't have as much success as I thought I would have, so I thought that maybe God didn't call me to write. That is when I made the executive decision to help other people write instead. I came up with a name, I started promoting, and even created a link for people to get on my calendar. I was so excited that I created an outline of how I could make $5000 a month if I met my goals. I started taking call after call, but then I heard God say "Stop. I didn't call you to get another job." I thought I heard Him wrong, so instead of fully shutting down, I just closed my calendar for a week. I wanted to hear that again because I knew that was wrong. I soon discovered that I heard that correctly; He did not want me to help people write. He told me, "that's not what I want you to do, I called me to write," This is where pride tried to rise up in me. I didn't want to go back and say I messed up and can no longer provide these services. I also didn't see how I would make money by being a writer and content creator. At this point, I had developed a close enough relationship with God, to cut my losses and follow him. This wasn't always true, for me but understanding that love isn't prideful made it an easier transition.

Choosing not to allow pride to take over taught me a valuable lesson. The plans that God has for me, are far greater than a $5000 a month job disguised as a business. Now, less than a year later, I am busier than ever and walking in purpose, but I had to fall on my sword. Now, if I would have asked about His will first, I wouldn't have gotten to this place. I say this to say His will is better. So, if He asks you to switch it up, you should really press into that. Your will is not better than His and we have to make sure we are not too prideful in life. Don't have so much pride in you that you ignore God.

It does not dishonor others; it is not self-seeking 1 Corinthians 13:5 NIV

Love doesn't dishonor anyone, and it is not all for self. I see a big theme here with God's definition of love. This love is not the selfish or conditional type. It is very risky. When you love this way, you do not dishonor others. I have seen many times where relationships end and both parties are spewing hate. The funny thing is that this is the same person that just last week they praised, they loved them so much, but now, due to some discovery or some "mistreatment," they hate each other and don't mind telling the world. This is so against what love is per God. I think they spew this dishonor to play the victim role to make it seem as though it isn't their fault. I have experienced this and from my experience the one talking the loudest is probably the one who brought the issues home. When God loves us, He doesn't do it for His own selfish desires. He also doesn't dishonor you or bring shame your way. He loves us all the same.

When you understand that God's love doesn't dishonor us, it becomes easier to discern God's voice in how we handle situations where we are hurt. A wise woman once told me that God exposes to heal and the enemy exposes to destroy. This statement really resonated with me, because I am a natural snooper. When I was going that rough season with my husband, I would go through everything phones and laptops included. I would try to convince myself I needed to know every detail about everything he did. I would declare that it was the only way to know the complete truth. When I started to snoop, I truly thought it was God, leading me to do this. After a couple of failed attempts at getting access to what I was looking for I would get the sense that God was saying "stop, I have told you what you need to know". I would ignore that because I was so determined and I just had to know everything, or so I thought. I soon learned no matter the degree of what I knew about my husband's indiscretions, during this time it all would lead to the same things, bitterness and rage. God truly knows the best way to bring truth or exposure. When God is doing it, it isn't to dishonor you.

Love is not self-seeking it means the act or practice of selfishly advancing one's own ends, according to the Merriam-Webster dictionary[F] (2020). When operating in love, you have to check your motives and do a heart check because the bible says God looks at the heart of the man. You cannot be loving to get your own selfish desires. On social media I see a lot of people saying I only love people who love me. If that is how you operate, you have it all wrong. If we wait on someone to love us, no one would ever feel God's love on this side of heaven. This love is one where it has to be genuine and from a good place. We can't love like God then run people away from God. This is why so many experience church hurt.

It is not easily angered 1 Corinthians 13:5 NIV

Love is not easily angered. This one I needed work on personally. As you can see, when someone hurts me, anger is my first reaction. I get extremely upset, which leads to other things that are not the fruit of the spirit. I want to be clear that it doesn't say you won't get angry, it said not easily angered. Everybody gets angry, even God. It takes repeated behaviors that aren't good that would lead to anger. I always think about how I deal with my bonus child. When I first started learning her, it was hard. She was two years old when we met and wasn't around much due to issues with her mother and father. By the time she came around more consistently she was about 6 years old. At that time, I didn't have kids that I birthed, so I was learning how to mother a six-year-old that I don't know. I expected certain things from her in how she acted. It was a source of frustration and anger. One day God started to get on me about how I spoke to her. I wasn't cursing her out, but my patience for her didn't exist at the time so I would get mad at her. That sounds ridiculous now, and it's not something I am happy about, but it's my truth. Over time God began to press on me and I started to feel His wrath. So, I decided to pray about the changes I needed to make.

With those changes my anger calmed down tremendously. I learned how to get her to understand me and me to understand her. Now, instead of expectation, I give her grace and corrected behaviors before I place expectation. I also rarely get angry with her, because the love I have shown her prevents a lot of problems. She is a very intelligent and well behaved eight-year-old these days. Of course, she is growing and learning but I have really grown in this area.

It keeps no record of wrongs 1 Corinthians 13:5 NIV

Love keeps no record of wrongs; this speaks to forgiveness. When you forgive someone, it's removing the charge you think they deserve. Not only removing it, but letting it go to the point you no longer bring it up in your memory bank or not to that person. So, when God loves us, He doesn't keep record of everything we did wrong or keep throwing it in our face. He meets us where we are, gives us grace, and exudes patience and kindness. This is the type of love we want other people to give us all the time. How many of us actually give this to other people, or ourselves, for that matter? As you grow in loving without condition, we have to remember to let our little black book of bad memories go.

Love does not delight in evil but rejoices with the truth. 1 Corinthians 13:6 NIV

Lord, as I wrote this part of the scripture, I had to repent because I have delighted in evil several times. It wasn't intentional, as in I wanted to see something bad but when something bad happens it gets the most attention. When something great happens; crickets. We have to be really careful about what we allow in our spirit. When I spend too much time on social media, I find myself delighting in the things of the world vs what God said. The second part of this is rejoicing in truth. Have you ever noticed that a lot of the things that draw us in are not really the truth? It's the part that entices you that keeps you there. When you rejoice in truth, you let go of evil. This piece of the scripture reminds me that evil can also translate into wrongdoing. So, we don't get excited about people doing wrong, but we do get excited when truth is exposed. We also know we don't battle with flesh and blood, so a lot of this evil we see is a straight spiritual battle and it's not really what we see. We won't delight in those things. When the truth shows up and prevails, we will indulge in it and get happy.

It always protects, always trusts, always hopes, always perseveres. 1 Corinthians 13:8 NIV

This is the part of the scripture I love the most because no matter what, God's love protects, trusts, hopes, and preserves. God always will love us no matter what we do or the condition of our circumstances. Why? Because this is His nature towards us, and He wants us to be like Him when dealing with our brothers and sisters. Love always wins in the end. Operating in love can really change a lot of situations that we face. One thing that I can appreciate about God is His love. Even when I didn't love Him, He loved me. When I was lost in the world, He continued to save me, protect me, trust me, have hope for me, and His love persevered me. So, I have seen God's love work in my life. The great thing about God is that He gives this to all his children no matter what condition you are in. There is nothing you can do to make Him take that away from you. It's important to God that we are like Him, so He gives love to bring us to Him by our own choice. He will never self-impose or manipulate us. The first part of 1 Corinthians 13:8 says love never fails. I promise it never fails.

After we learn what God's love is, we need to understand what we are supposed to do with that love. He didn't go into this much detail just to let us know that's how He loves us; He wants us to do something with this love and in the way described in Matthew 22:37:

Jesus replied: "'Love the Lord your God with all your heart and with all your soul and with all your mind.' [a] 38 This is the first and greatest commandment. Matthew 22:37

In His word God tells us we are called to do a lot of things, but the greatest command is love. This is the biggest mandate that we have. We are to love the Lord with all our heart. Once we love God like this it will overflow into loving everyone including ourselves. Before I truly knew the love of God, when I was younger, I would always declare "I love people, like God loves you but that's it". I use this blanket statement to try to illustrate that there were no romantic feelings involved or even a strong liking for them. Little did I know I was declaring a powerful statement. I didn't understand love in so much detail like I do know, so in a sense I was lying. I meant to say I cared about their well-being and not that I actually loved them. I didn't love like Christ until after I was married. I had a very contingent, conditional type of love. I did not even understand how important this was in the body of Christ. Loving someone like God said is literally lifesaving.

My command is this: Love each other as I have loved you John 15:12 NIV

After our first commandment on love we are called to love each other how He has loved us. Whew, just the thought of that can seem scary. God is a complete risk tasker when He loves us. He loves us knowing we may fail, mess up, hurt Him, make Him upset and outright deny Him. None of that matters to Him. He loves us so much that His biggest concern is our wellbeing. He wants us to know we can always come to Him, even in our mistakes. He wants us to show other people His love through us. His love will allow us to help lead people to Him when they are lost. While being married, I grew tired of my husband. I wanted to leave but God continued to tell me it wasn't His will. I do my best to be obedient, so I was grieved at first. Over time I learned how much God loved me and how I needed to love my husband in the midst of what he was doing. No matter what I felt, God needed me to help save him in a sense. I knew I couldn't save him, but I could show God's love through me. Let me tell you, in the beginning he thought it was manipulation. He wouldn't say that I was manipulating him, but he showed that. It was hard to stand in the gap for him. I did it because I knew how God's love had changed me and I wanted to be obedient. I didn't do it because I wanted to make him treat me right. Well in the beginning I did, and I quickly changed directions. My motive had to be for him to come to God. This is where that self-seeking part came in. When I think about the love definition, I had a hard time with motives. So, we are called to love others, but it has to be done per the definition in 1 Corinthians or it will not be done correctly.

And the second is like it: 'Love your neighbor as yourself.' Matthew 22:39 NIV

When I was first introduced to reading the bible, I took a lot of the words at face value, meaning I didn't study and ask for revelation. I just read it and it went right on out. When I first read it, I just heard I love your neighbor. I never focused on the self-part. I honestly thought loving yourself wasn't important. I thought our only mandate was to love other people. As I grew in love, I began to really understand that I should love as I love myself. I realized the reason I struggled with love is because I didn't love myself. So, I was loving them from my level of love. I realized that I could never love other people if I didn't love myself. Honestly, I didn't love myself at all and neither did I love other people. I had to really understand the importance how we love ourselves. If I didn't love myself correctly, there was no way I could love people properly.

CHAPTER IV
HOW LOVING MYSELF LOOKED IN MY LIFE

Growing up, I just didn't like myself at all. I didn't love me. I actually hated myself. I didn't value my thoughts, my ambitions or anything else. Growing up I was always told how pretty I was and that I should model. I ignored those compliments because I didn't think I was pretty. My definition of pretty came from attention and how your body looked. Yes, my face was pretty but due to being bigger than most of my classmates I didn't really feel like I was beautiful. The earliest memory of me realizing I wasn't the same size as other kids happened in 4th grade. I was in class and there was this boy who didn't care for me. We were arguing, and he called me chubby. I was so hurt I cried and hid under the desk. The teacher had to get me from under there. I was ashamed. That day I told my mother, and she reassured me that I wasn't. It didn't matter because his words became my inner voice. It didn't matter how many positive compliments I got because this one set in me, and I believed it.

Over the years, the thoughts I had about myself that showed I didn't love myself increased. As I think about this, I believe it was a trick to decrease my confidence so I could hide behind someone I felt looked better than me. My lack of self-love looked like people pleasing, perfection, and the comparison game. I desperately wanted to be liked by people and I wanted to look perfect because I had so many insecurities. I didn't want that to be exposed, so I wore a mask majority of my life. I couldn't risk being found out. So, what people called me being nice or sweet really were me looking for love and acceptance in places I shouldn't have been looking.

I remember being in the second grade having a boyfriend. He asked me to be his girlfriend and he was the most disruptive boy in class. I felt good about this, I even gave him my number knowing I knew better. I liked the feeling of being liked at this age. Honestly, I always had some little boy "liking" me. This is what made me feel love or what I thought I loved. Over time he wasn't my boyfriend, and he liked another girl. I liked him so much I helped him get with the girl who was my neighbor. I wanted to please him no matter what the cost was. This is where my people pleasing started, in my opinion. I was willing to sacrifice whatever to make you happy. I needed everyone to like me. The minute someone didn't like me it became a huge problem.

I remember there was a new student, and she befriended me first. The thing about new students is they don't know your position of hierocracy in the class. I was friends with a little of everyone but wasn't that popular; maybe because of my own self-esteem. I wanted to impress her, so I introduced her to the popular kids as my friend. She befriended a girl that was my best friend. They got closer than me and the new girl. I was hurt, so I started acting out in school. I gave my teacher a hard time. I also started doing questionable things. One time I wrote in a notebook that no one should steal my notebook, or I was going to hurt them. I was filled with anger as a child. I wanted someone to just love and care for me, so this was one way I tried to love me. I worked off the words and liking of other people. I also wanted to avoid anything that would hurt like teasing or fighting. I was afraid of being disliked, although I disliked myself.

People pleasing started there and continued throughout my adult life. Even if I disagreed or couldn't do something, I made myself do it. It didn't matter the consequence it had in my personal life. I also allowed other people to determine what I did. I remember the first time I skipped school. I was in the 8th grade. I had never done that before, but my friends convinced me we would have a good time and it would all be ok. It went way left and people's lives were sent in a different direction as a result.

The idea to not go to school came from someone older than I was who invited me, and I invited a friend my age to come along. We made an elaborate plan; I paid my brother off not to tell on me and we did it. We went to a house with men over 20 years old. My two friends were sexually active, I wasn't. When we got there, men were everywhere, and the house, for the most part, was bare. There were adults everywhere. As I reflect, it was a dope house. These men had a sister so we all three kind of stuck by her. I was so afraid but couldn't show that because I couldn't take the mask off. I was supposed to be a rebel at this time; I wasn't. While there, people were having sex and doing lines of cocaine. I was strong enough to say no to these things. The men would have sex with one then the next one. It was a lot, so I went outside during most of the encounters. I just made it clear I was a virgin; I was terrified and couldn't hide it. That day we made it home and didn't get caught.

Afterwards I was glad, but then they wanted to go back over there. See, I didn't know a lot about the enemy, so he was pulling all of us in that direction. Because I couldn't stand my ground, we all lied to our parents and went over on a day we were out of school. I was so silly; I took my little brother with me. I was told there would be a child there. We got over there and this time it was different. The energy was different, things were more chaotic. It wasn't as fun as I felt like it was. I wanted to leave, but my "friends" wouldn't tell me how to get back. I was hurt and scared because my brother was with me and he was like 7 at the time maybe younger. I decided I would just walk until I figured it out, I couldn't stay, all I could think about was something happening to my brother. Thank God, one of the men told me how to get there and walked me to the short cut. We got home, and I thought we were safe and didn't get caught. I decided I wasn't doing that anymore at least not with my brother.

That night, the parents of the friend I invited started calling me. My friend didn't come home, neither did the other girl. They really put me in a bad position. My mother wasn't home, so I thought I was in the clear. The next morning, she still wasn't there, so I told on myself because that girl mama was coming. She came and not only told about the day before but also about us skipping school. Then my brother told on me. My world was crashing all because I wanted to please people. This situation was so embarrassing it got around the school and my teachers started holding me accountable for my friend. These two girls ended up running away a lot after this incident. My family came down so hard on me about this. I was told how bad I was, how grown I was, and how fast I was. I really needed help, but they didn't know how to help me.

My people pleasing continued, I just became sneakier because I also was a perfectionist. I always wanted my mother's approval on everything. So, if anything didn't match her standards I either hid it or took care of it. This started as a child. I remember all the times I did something and blamed my younger brother because he couldn't defend himself. Then at school, if I got a bad progress report or detention, I would sign for my mother. I couldn't bare her being mad at me. I was already a mess at home, I had to get something right and school had to be it. I always felt I wasn't good enough for her. School was the one way I could get praise. I stayed on the honor roll or principal's list. I got involved with a lot of things just to prove my worth. It had to be perfect if it wasn't, I couldn't present that to her. I was afraid of her disapproval because I thought she wouldn't love me anymore. I now understand that's not true, but as a child that was all I could equate to love.

My perfection came a lot from comparing. I always felt like I had to compete with my siblings and people at school. So, if someone made principal's list I would be upset because I made honor roll instead. I didn't think I was good enough. I remember I took a test, and it said I read on the 4th grade reading level and I was in the 11th grade. I was so embarrassed I fought with my teacher and told her the test was wrong. I convinced her that it couldn't be right. I was a great writer, but I wasn't much of a reader. I skim read, and I used cliff notes when they gave us books. I could read but I didn't comprehend much. It took me a few times before I understood what I read. Learning that the students in my class didn't have that problem made me feel unworthy. I worked hard to be free for 12th grade. I was over school because my issues started to show, I couldn't hide that I had a comprehension problem. I was a great test taker, so I easily covered this all these years. I also was a strong writer so not comprehending could easily be covered.

The comparison game flooded over into my social life. I wanted to be rebellious like other girls. See, by seventeen I was done trying to make my mother happy. I realized there was nothing I could do, so I rebelled very hard against her. I stopped coming home a lot and skipped school at least 2 times a week in 12th grade. I wanted to be free in a sense, so I spent a lot of time with men and my best friend. We skipped together we both were dealing with our own identity and worth issues. Familiar spirits will always link and by this time I was having sex with men. These men had schedules that worked with school hours. So, to run from one of the places that showed my insecurities I spent a lot of time away from it. Luckily, I worked hard from 9th to 11th grade so I still graduated. I really got into a lot of things during this time including experimenting with marijuana.

At this time, I didn't realize that's how I showed myself love. Yes, I said it. I thought I needed people in order to experience love. So, pleasing people and trying to be like people seemed to be the only thing that worked. Also, I thought love was supposed to hurt so the sacrifices I had to make came with the territory. These things lingered for a very long time. Sometimes I have to check myself to make sure I am not falling back into these habits. For example, when I started advocating for HIV, I was drawn to a lot of other people who advocated. Originally, I was upset with God because he asked me to do something so many other people already did. I spent a lot of time comparing myself to them and refusing to support and connect because I wanted my own thing. After I started to get delivered from these things, I realized I see them because I need to serve them. There is an attack among women not working together and I have been charged to change the narrative. I learned that these things will block you from your calling and purpose. That's why it's important we love ourselves and others. Love doesn't envy.

After I realized how I loved myself, I realized some of my bigger struggles had a lot to do with my self-esteem and holding onto unforgiveness. I was that girl who was vengeful, you hurt me I'm going to hurt you ten times worse. This showed up in my friendships, my relationships and my family. I was someone who wanted people to please me how I did them. When they didn't, I told myself they were mean and deserved how I treated them.

My best friend and I have been through some stuff due to both of us needing growth and healing. I remember her being pregnant and me supposing to help her do something pertaining to the baby. On the way there, I went to the wrong house and although I could have just rerouted, I decided not to show. She acted like she was ok, but she wasn't. So, I moved on and continued to be her friend. I noticed she stopped talking to me. I called one day, and she had the baby. She was so dry with me. I was hurt and felt like she was so wrong. I couldn't see where I wasn't operating in love and being understanding. So, I made a conscious decision to never call her again. I was no longer her friend. I couldn't stand her, and I said some awful things about her and her child. I confessed all of this so I can talk about it now. When she reached out, I acted like nothing happened. We eventually resolved our issues, but this was the type of friend I was. We're only friends as long as you bow down to me, it didn't matter what I did to you. I never would accept responsibility. This looked uglier in relationships because I would do things to embarrass the men I felt did me wrong.

When my first relationship was ending post diagnosis, I felt I needed to get him back. I would tell him I was going to school to study for my nursing test. He would drop me off and I would ride the train to get back for him to pick me up. What I was really doing was dating other men. I was having park dates, movie dates and all. I started going to more clubs to show him that he was missing out on all this while he was trying to control me and cheating on me every chance he got. Around him, I couldn't express myself, so I walked on eggshells and made him feel like all was well. One day all that came to an end, and he knew my real emotions.

One night I went out with my best friends. I ate around 8:00pm, we left and started drinking around 11:00pm. Before I made it into the club and was extremely wasted. When we got inside, the music was great and I danced, which I really don't do. Then I began to buy drinks. I had at least four mixed drinks, I did eat something then I ended up having a beer. Before I knew it, I was in and out of consciousness. I really didn't understand where

I was or what was going on. My friends placed me on a coach next to someone else that was just like me. The room was spinning, and I wanted to just sleep. After some time had passed, I heard my friends voice.

-"Ok, let us help you"
-"No, I am ok" I said in a drunken and sleep state.

I remember everyone asking if I needed help and telling us to hurry up so we wouldn't get in trouble for public intoxication. I really don't know how I made it to the car but I knew that the driver was used to this me. When I was younger, she took us to prom where I got messed up on drugs and alcohol. I was legit embarrassed, but too drunk to think about it. I fell asleep on the twenty-minute ride. I sort of remember them having to pull over for me to throw up. Did I? I'm not quite sure. Once we got to my apartment, they helped me up the stairs. That night I wore a dress, and I had my girdle on under it. We walked in and my ex-boyfriend came out the back; the sight of him made me mad. I took off my dress and laid on the floor. In the background I heard talking.

-"You need to help her" my best friend shouted.
-"I'm gone run some bath water"

I looked at my ex and I said some of the nastiest and hateful things to him. I made it clear that I didn't need his help and he should leave me alone. Right after, I began to throw up. It was a bad night and the next day I was sick. I had vomit in my hair. I was so embarrassed.

My pent-up words and anger came out in ways I didn't want it to. This is because I harbored my real emotions behind my need to feel love in my life. I wanted it so badly that I accepted whatever you threw at me. Overtime, I learned that I needed true deliverance in order to love myself the way 1 Corinthians 13 expressed it. I needed to not be vengeful, but first I had to deal with my unforgiveness.

"In prayer there is a connection between what God does and what you do. You can't get forgiveness from God, for instance, without also forgiving others. If you refuse to do your part, you cut yourself off from God's part. Matthew 6:14-15 MSG

The reason I was so hard on other people and had high expectations because I couldn't forgive people yet alone myself. I felt that somehow me holding onto unforgiveness I could control the narrative. I soon learned that people continue to live while you over there pouting about what they did yesterday or last year. They made peace with it. I also learned that by me holding that charge against them I was only hurting myself. I was the one angry all the time. Me not forgiving showed in everything I did. I really hated men at one point because of the charges I held against my father, my uncle and the men I choose to date. I had to be willing to forgive them because it blocked my blessing from God, and this is the most important relationship we have. I had to forgive everyone including me. It was harder to forgive myself because I felt like I didn't deserve it. I had made a lot of mistakes and allowed so many people to walk all over me. In a sense I took revenge out on myself. Holding onto it was holding myself accountable. It also stopped me from loving myself properly.

I used to feel like I didn't deserve good things in my life. I didn't deserve to be in nursing school or to become a nurse. God was choosing me, qualifying me, but I didn't deserve any of that from Him. I was a bad child. I had to learn that you don't have to deserve forgiveness to get forgiven. If this was done on the basis of who deserves it according to the world, none of us could experience true forgiveness that leads to repentance.

Don't hit back; discover beauty in everyone. If you've got it in you, get along with everybody. Don't insist on getting even; that's not for you to do. "I'll do the judging," says God. "I'll take care of it." Romans 12:17-19. MSG

My unforgiveness led me to take matters into my own hands; another mistake a lot of us make. We think we have to fix everything when God will fix everything. He says He will take care of all of our issues for us we just have to let Him do it. When we do it in our own strength, He won't do it. God is the only one who can get true repentance. There is nothing you can do or say to make someone understand what they did. God has to change their hearts.

When I began to have issues in the realm of marriage, I desperately needed my husband to feel my wrath vs. God's wrath. I used to feel like God was too nice to him. I needed to make him feel me. I was horrible. It's true, two wrongs will never make a right. When you allow yourself to fall into things that are not like God, you do more damage and it's easy to trick you. The enemy would trick me into thinking things were way bigger than what they really were. This led to me reacting in crazy ways. I remember one day my husband and I got into it. I got in the shower and when I came out, he was gone. I assumed a woman picked him up. I was so mad; I destroyed our whole house. I broke sentimental things we could never get back. I broke stuff then barricaded myself in a room. I didn't know the influence of a wife at the time.

The wise woman builds her house, but with her own hands the foolish one tears hers down. Proverbs 14:1 NIV

I was literally tearing my house down. When my husband got back, his anger was bad because I hurt him. Although he was deserving in my opinion, it still hurt. Seeing him hurt, hurt me worse than the trick I fell for. It was a bad day in my household.

I never was taught how to be a wife and I still was fighting to be loved by him when really God's love was free. God's love wasn't good enough for me. It wasn't a tangible type of love like what I thought it should be. My low self-esteem started to show as well.

A lot of my issues stemmed from my own belief about myself. I really looked at myself like I was almost good enough. When dealing with men, I felt as though I had to take what I got. One example is if I met someone online or over the phone, my concern was always if they liked me. It didn't matter if I liked them because I would settle. I wanted them to like me though. I needed to be liked at least enough to have sex. I learned that the link to sex in love related deeply to my love languages. Even as a married woman, if my husband didn't express his pleasure, I thought he didn't like it and I wasn't satisfying him. If he denied me, it meant he didn't want me.

But you are a chosen people, a royal priesthood, a holy nation, God's special possession, that you may declare the praises of him who called you out of darkness into his wonderful light. 1 Peter 2:9 NIV

It's important that we first learn who we are in Christ. What does God say about us, because that is our true identity. I developed my self-esteem issues from myself and the world around me. The world around told me I always fell short in everything. So, I assumed this identity. When I discovered I was failing as a wife, in my opinion this exacerbated my feelings and for the first time in life I had to look in the mirror and figure out what was missing, what was wrong, and this is how I really started loving me. Starting to love myself led me to realize I had these issues in me. During the roughest season of my marriage, I learned to love myself.

CHAPTER V
HOW LOVING MYSELF LOOKED IN MY LIFE

Shortly after marriage I realized that my oh so perfect husband wasn't oh so perfect. I originally didn't want to do anything to fix it. I didn't want to work on it because I felt I should have known better. The problem was that I was suffering from idolatry. When you idolize something or someone God will show you who they really are. Also being this way, you turn from God's love. See, God still loves you, but you become dependent on the love from other people. It's nothing wrong with loving people and people loving you, but if you don't have God's love you will find it difficult, as I have, in life. I had to snatch off band aids and allow real healing to happen. The healing I needed had nothing to do with my husband. God used this situation to teach me how to love properly. What some may not understand is that God loves us the way He does and to the magnitude He does to bring us to Him and lead us to repentance.

Those who cling to worthless idols turn away from God's love for them. Jonah 2:8. NIV

I began to learn about different love languages soon after marriage. I learned that we all understand love differently. So, what I feel is love may not be how you feel love. There are five basic love languages; physical touch, acts of service, quality time, gifts and words of affirmation. Through reading, it's not hard to see that words of affirmation and physical touch are mine. I wasn't getting this as a child, so I leaned more into physical touch. This is why I needed sex from such a young age because that's how physical touch was introduced to me. I learned now that things like hugs, and hand holding make me feel loved to. Words of affirmation are important to me as well. So, to communicate love to myself I spend a lot of time speaking positively about myself to myself. I also like to get massages and things like that. So, I can in a sense feel it. I also like to set the atmosphere so I can feel God's presence. As I showed myself more love, I could show that to other people.

After I understood how I understood love, I studied the definition of love and started implementing that into my life. Some parts were easier than others. Some took more healing than others. It was easy for me to do things and be kind to myself but harder to have patience. It was definitely hard to forgive myself for all the things I had done. But, I did it. It was also hard to not be envious and compare myself. I was so hard on myself in the past. I told myself all kinds of untrue things. For example, I would say I should have known better about certain things that I was never taught.

Sometimes we are our own worst critic when we have to literally love ourselves. Sometimes I hate that it took for things to literally crash around me for God to get my attention. Honestly, I didn't know the importance of loving myself. I grew up in a society where you come last. You help other people, forgive them and take care of them. But there is an unwritten rule that makes us feel like we absolutely cannot care for ourselves. I am here to tell you this is false, and we have to switch up the narrative. We can love just like Christ, starting with us. We also have to remember we are a spiritual being having a human experience. Therefore, we have to take care of both parts of us.

Self-care is a very popular word that we say, but are we really caring for ourselves. As women, we want to help everyone and everybody and we end up putting ourselves last. Even when we discuss order, we say God, family and then career. Where do we fall in that order? We should fall somewhere around family, but we think about the other people. We find ourselves burned out and creating bad habits. We have to care for ourselves so we can properly do the work that we are called to. When we neglect ourselves, we find ourselves burnout, hurting and unable to do the work we are called to. There is only so much that one can take before they literally run out of steam.

When I was first introduced to the word of self-care, I thought very surface level. I thought it just included getting my nails done, keep my hair down and shop. At the time I couldn't do these things due to lack of funds, so I thought I needed to make time and put money to the side. As I reflect, I realized that even when I was able to afford these things, I wasn't caring for myself. These things relieved stress immediately and made me feel good but it wasn't taking care of me. I had to look deeper than what I heard. God started to lead me to podcasts and things that took this myth out of my head. When I first wanted to talk about this, it would have been things such as the ones listed. I have grown a lot in love within the last year or so. I want you to understand that self-care is deeper than that.

According to the Fort Gary Women's Resource Center self-care is "is care provided "for you, by you." It's about identifying your own needs and taking steps to meet them. It is taking the time to do some activities that nurture you. Self-care is about

taking proper care of yourself and treating yourself as kindly as you treat others [9]*.*"

Self-care is how you care for yourself and in what areas you need care. Thinking about how I care for other people in my life, most people are drawn to me because of my encouragement and realistic strategies to get the things we want and need out of life. Not one person has come to me because I could paint their nails or do their hair. They really are in desperate need of direction; something I had to learn the hard way. I am not someone that's very teachable. I think this is because I am very analytical and need to know how you arrived at such an answer and most people don't want to go that deep with me. I usually end up going to college when I need growth in an area. So, we understand that self-care is about discovering what your needs are and meeting those needs yourself.

I discovered that self-care to me is journaling, praying and fasting. I needed to be spiritually fed properly to make sure I wasn't leaning into my own understanding. These three things that are how I make direct connection to God. When I start my day without prayer and journaling, I find myself all over the place. Also, taking spiritual feeding further, I listen to podcasts that cater to the growing Christian these days. As I grew in my walk, the things I did to make sure I stayed connected to the source looked different. When I began this journey, it looked like a lot of sermon watching and church going. It also looked like me serving a lot in the church because it gave me a sense of fulfillment. By serving, it gave me something I needed to care for me. It was my thing that had nothing to do with my family or my job. It was what I needed to care for myself. I needed people in my corner who understood God the way I did and who were spiritually stronger.

I'm not here to tell you what self-care is to you because, as you see, it's what you make it. What do you need to do to be properly cared for? The key word is self, what you do need to do to care for you. Since that all can look different for various people, I want to talk about somethings we need to establish that will make it easier to be able to provide the self-care we need. Sometimes we need to make sure that we deal with the things that can prevent us from caring for ourselves. I also want to show you why it's important as it relates to love.

One of the biggest things we need to establish is boundaries. This is so hard for most of us because we've never established them. We mistake loving someone for being a pushover. We thought we had to manipulate when we didn't. We thought loving them meant not having to set boundaries.

Like a city whose walls are broken through, is a person who lacks self-control. Proverbs 25:28 NIV

In other versions it's says the one who lacks control over their spirit. In the scripture a person who has no control over themselves is a city whose walls are broken through. I want you to think of boundaries as your borders. So, if you have no borders the people next to you can walk right on in. They won't even know they are wrong because you haven't put anything up. But once it happens, you will be upset because you thought they should see the walls you hadn't built. There is no law against creating boundaries; we have to do this to be able to take care of ourselves. An example of this for me was when my morning routine began to take longer.

I would get annoyed with my family when they didn't understand. You know why they didn't understand? I hadn't opened my mouth, and I was waking up too late. So, now I wake up early so I can get my time with God without distraction. My family also understands that I need this time in the morning. This isn't a choice; it's as much needed as exercise and eating breakfast. It is our responsibility to put these in place whether that boundary needs to be coming on your side or with your family. Now I get asked if I prayed. See, your family will catch on when you take care of you. Guess what? They also get the benefits. When I don't do my routine, my husband can tell. He encourages me to do what I need to do and is very selfless. Once self-care is important to you it will become important to everyone around you. We need to make it a routine and not a one-off thing. We routinely care for everyone else including the dog.

"Very early in the morning, while it was still dark, Jesus got up, left the house and went off to a solitary place, where he prayed." - Mark 1:35 NIV

Jesus did everything for everybody, including himself. He went off and prayed alone. This scripture was one-way He cared for himself. If he didn't do this, I'm sure it could have led to the same frustrations we experienced. He got up early because no one else would likely be up giving Him this time where people were least expecting Him. It became a routine for Him, because it was necessary to finish the work of our Father. Imagine how Jesus would have been if he only did it one time in all the years He served. I could see a burnt out, upset, and addicted Jesus. When we allow things to stress us out all the time, it can be related to not routinely caring for us. We all have a stop button and some of us find it the hard way.

While working as a nurse, I spent an eight-year career caring for many patients and neglecting my own self. The last few months of working were the hardest ever in my life. When I was leaving, I blamed everyone except the fact was that I didn't establish boundaries and once I did it was too late. I was already losing my mind. As a nurse, we sometimes get upset with the nurse who says I'm not taking patients over the safe number. I was someone who would take the patient and just suck it up. Months of doing this take a toll on you. Maybe three months before leaving I was told I was getting a new patient. I refused because I just discharged someone, and I was already four hours behind on my other patients. The patient who left was very sick and was going to another facility. If you work in the healthcare field, you understand this. My manager had no sympathy, all he knew was we needed the next patient. He refused to take the patient. I got so upset I went to the bathroom and cried. I was losing my mind.

After that incident I calmed down and moved on. It happened two days later, and I really lost my mind. I couldn't take it and wrote a two weeks' notice. Before I could turn it in, I got pneumonia. Now, we know I have HIV so yes, I can get sick easier, but my meds were fine. The problem wasn't my HIV, it was a buildup of stress and then within a month after I got sick again. I had to get out of there. As much as I loved it, bedside nursing drove me out of my mind. I had to go. I do believe this was used for His good because it was overdue. I know He saved me from being wrongly admitted into a mental ward. I was over capacity in my mind and my lack of boundaries at work and a lack of a self-care routine played a role. It is important that as you get more self-care in your life, that you establish these two things.

Now what does all this have to do with loving yourself? Let's go back to the definition of love. Love is kind, it always protects, always perseveres, doesn't boast, and it doesn't envy. If you don't care for yourself spiritually and physically it can be easy to be failing to do these things for yourself. As you want to increase the love you have for yourself, you have to show yourself actual love. Self-care is just one of the ways that play a huge role. As you care for you, caring for others will become natural. Have you caught on that a lot of things stem from you? It all starts with how you think and act and what you know. You get what you allow. If you don't establish the rules of engagement someone else will do it. I remember when I didn't love myself, I shrunk a lot. I would know how to help, how to do something, know that something was wrong, but I would never speak. I didn't want to speak up and be wrong. This is where perfectionism played a role. Eventually I realized by not opening my mouth I suffered and so did the people who needed my voice.

By creating self-care and increasing the love I had for me, I changed significantly. I was now physically showing myself that I mattered, and someone cared for me, and that person was me next to God. I no longer needed someone here on earth to love me because I loved me. I loved myself so much that I now could teach people how to love me. It felt great. I no longer had to accept people yelling at me or telling me what I could and couldn't do. I didn't have to sacrifice my obedience. One thing I do is fast every Wednesday. I do it so much that now my husband knows not to try and tell me I need to eat. My family that lives close by tries their best to let me be on that day. They know I am fasting, praying and recording the Queen Redeemed Podcast. They already know I am not even here in this realm. It's possible to love you and take care of you without feeling guilty. It takes YOU to step up and establish what needs to happen.

I remember when I first started to understand the concept, I didn't really know what it was to take care of me. I grew up taking care of people my whole life and never me. When I was younger, I always helped my grandmother. Then at eleven I started to babysit children which I sacrificed most of my childhood to do. I didn't even take care of myself when I should have been careless. Then I was the oldest so at home, so I had to handle a lot of things including managing our home cooking by age twelve. I was washing all the clothes in the house by age seven. The concept of fun or caring for myself was foreign to me. I had to look within and see what I needed in order to interact and be an active participant in life.

I would start within when deciding on doing self-care. I would also look at what is causing you to feel uneasy. For some, that's not having a savings account or unpaid bills. Also, some people need to take social media breaks because social media can overwhelm you. I realized a few years ago I have to take frequent breaks from Facebook. Why? Because I advocate for HIV and my timeline has a lot of that on it. In my personal life I'm not constantly reminded that I am living with something I don't want and the issues we all have to deal with. Self-care is different for all of us, so while having a savings account may not be an act of self-care for you, it may be for other people. This is a very individualized process and it's important that you look within and decide what taking care of yourself looks like.

When you don't care for yourself you aren't loving yourself. When you don't love yourself, you could possibly forget about caring for yourself. When I needed my husband to feel love, I was depressed, angry, hurt, envious and vengeful. Nothing like the true definition of Agape love. This showed in my daily life, so do you think I was loving other people right? No. I think about all the times I was essentially rude to his friends because I thought he was being fake. When they visited, I wouldn't come out the room because I was dealing with shame and embarrassment. The perception of who I was, was different than who I actually was. I had a lot of rectifying to do to rebuild relationships. That's something you must remember as well. As you grow in love and get healed, the damage also has to be repaired.

I reflect back over my life and realize that if I would have taken time when I was alone to get to know me and love me, it would have saved me so much heartache. I don't regret going through because now I can help you get through by writing this book. I can help you love on yourself more and understand how important self-care is. I never knew that love was this important but it's the key to things like deliverance and breakthrough. We have to treat ourselves correctly, so we can get to the place that God has for us. Life is a journey and we make our journeys hard sometimes due to a lack of knowledge. So, if you find yourself lacking one or both of these it's time to do some self-assessments around love and self-care. Caring and loving you is the one thing that will allow you to overflow and stay in the overflow.

CHAPTER VI
LOVING INTO PURPOSE

As a follower in Christ and a believer in God it's important to know that God has a purpose for everything he does. He didn't put us down here because he just needed companions and dolls. He created everything with a purpose. The biggest thing that we all find hard at one point or another is knowing what our purpose is. We think it's one thing and may discover it's another thing. One thing I do know is that without proper love for you it makes it so much harder. Before we go deeper let me share a story with you.

"Before I formed you in the womb I knew you, before you were born I set you apart; I appointed you as a prophet to the nations. Jeremiah 1:5 NIV

When I went to college, I originally wanted to be a writer period. I had no other things I felt passionate about. I have been writing longer than I can remember. I got to college and my uncle told me I had a few choices none of them included writing. I wasn't disappointed because he convinced me that I needed to pick something that would make me a lot of money. This was the same uncle I couldn't forgive so you know I was rebellious. So, originally, I complied and went to school because he said he would pay but actually he did a loan and cosigned.

After I started, I realized I didn't want to do any of those courses he suggested, but he had a point I needed to make real money, so writing wasn't an option. I also didn't want to lose my passion for it. I decided to pick nursing. It made sense because I been caring for everybody my whole life anyway. I did this did well worked, and it drove me crazy. After two years I realized I wasn't destined to work for people but out of comfort I stayed, depressed and all. See at that time I didn't have boundaries, standards or love for myself at the core. I was ok sacrificing my sanity for money. Honestly many of us do that. At least 80% of people dislike their jobs. We have become ok with getting paid an hourly wage and making sure bills get paid vs walking into the purpose God called us to.

I believe our problems start because we lack love. As we grow in love, we will seek out our purpose.

When I started loving me, I knew my days were numbered in Corporate America. It was like a light switch went off in my head and me helping someone build their dream cost me a lot when it came time to do what I was called to. When I wrote my first book I was elated and excited. The next week I went to work unfulfilled. I changed my shift and location thinking it would help. It got worse and within two months I was over it. I couldn't focus on what I was called to while working that job. It demanded my time while I was there and away from there. Not only was I not able to fully love me I couldn't love my family. All the stress at work came home with me. It played a huge role in my marriage suffering. I had to make a conscious decision to figure out what I was really called to.

I knew that if it was nursing it couldn't be in the capacity I was working. I had developed horrible habits during this time, I wasn't caring for myself and I didn't take care of me. Due to that I couldn't walk into the purpose God called me to. As you love yourself more and dig deeper with God, you will crave your purpose and it will become clearer and clearer to you.

Many are the plans in a person's heart, but it is the LORD's purpose that prevails. Proverbs 19:21 NIV

The definition of purpose is that which a person sets before himself as an object to be reached or accomplished; the end or aim to which the view is directed in any plan, measure or exertion. In this definition it's important to add than as a believer our purposes are determined before we get here. We spend a long time trying to figure out exactly, what God called us here to do on earth. If we think about the basic definition of purpose, you see that it is what a person goes after as an object to be reached. As a believer we have to learn our purposes from God. We didn't create ourselves. The simplest way to create an analogy for this is like when we pick and choose a dog. Before getting the dog, you decide what you need the dog for and what qualities they need to have. In my life I got another dog because my first dog needed a playmate. Now, we only have the dog we got as a companion. Now, we expect her to protect us, but she doesn't. We want another dog and we can't get one because she doesn't get alone with other dogs. Although we tried to change her purpose, we couldn't because her purpose in our lives is already established.

So, this is how we have to look at purposes in our lives. God has called you to do something actually more than one thing in my opinion and that is the only thing that you can focus on. Now the difference in us discovering purpose is that although we are born with purpose, we don't come out knowing that. This is because we are born into a world that we are not of. We have to take the proper steps to learn more about your purpose. The first step in this is love because without love there is no purpose. As you accept God's love for you, and you love you the longing for purpose will rise up in you.

We know that love leads to purpose, but how do we get there? This is a question I always get. Nakeisa, how did you know your purpose? The answer is I didn't know, and I get more revelations as time goes on. The first step to discovering my purpose was asking God.

Ask, and it shall be given you; seek, and ye shall find; knock, and it shall be opened unto you:8 For every one that asked receiveth; and he that speaketh findeth; and to him that knocketh it shall be opened. Matthew 7:7-8. KJV

In life we miss the mark because we don't understand that we can ask for whatever we need from God. We will go a pray a church down, pray a conference down but we will not ask for what we need. Then when and if we do, we are timid. We have to boldly go and put his word back on him. In Matthew 7:7 he said ask and it shall be given. So, ask and ask boldly about what for what you need from him. I remember when we I started to ask God to have, I talked to him about certain things. I realized that I had not asked God about several things. I had to start writing down what I needed to discuss with God in prayer. This was the beginning of my newfound prayer life. Initially, some answers came through and then I started getting stuck. I couldn't figure out why? I thought I was asking. This is how I learned God meets us where we are. I started hearing I needed to fast.

"And when you fast, don't make it obvious, as the hypocrites do, for they try to look miserable and disheveled so people will admire them for their fasting. I tell you the truth, that is the only reward they will ever get. 17 But when you fast, comb your hair[a] and wash your face. 18 Then no one will notice that you are fasting, except your Father, who knows what you do in private. And your Father, who sees everything, will reward you. Matthew 6:16-18 NLT

Fasting is all over the bible and as you read the stories you realize that it's always coupled with praying. When you fast, you deny your flesh to focus on an area that you feel led to do. For some it's how they hear God the clearest. I used to fast with churches when I was younger. I never saw the fruits of those fast because I was so focused on eating that I didn't even know if God was talking. All I could think about was eating when the time came. I was more so just starving myself. The first time I fasted with intention was for my marriage. I was in a group of standers who were doing a short fast to gain clarity. For the first time I heard God speak to me. I thought maybe it was me, but I realized it was him. He spoke the words restoration over my life and marriage. At the time I didn't understand it, but I knew that I shouldn't be quick to leave my husband. It took a lot more fasting and a lot more praying, but I started getting the answers I was seeking. So, as you seek your purpose and to understand it you have to incorporate intentional fasting. Just because you didn't eat until 5pm doesn't mean you are fasting in the way God wants you to. Fasting God's way is all about consecration and gaining insight. When I do my weekly fast, I keep my ears and heart open because God tells me what I need to do and how it needs to be done. He really manages my whole entire life because I allow him to. As we grow in fasting and prayer we have to learn about mediations.

Meditation is waiting on responses from God. Meditation has become perverted and people use it in ways that are not biblical. When I say this word I literally mean listening to God. When I first left my job to become a full-time entrepreneur, all I wanted was money. I wasn't trying to discover no purpose I just knew that I left my job, but money is needed to survive. I tried all kinds of things to make money. I was praying and fasting, but I wasn't waiting on a response from God. Yes, God responds to us straight forward, but we like popcorn prayers. We make them so religious and we don't like to write and hold conversation. If we treated him like the Father He is, we could get more clarity and more answers.

One day I was at home just frustrated because, yet again, something I put a lot of work into wasn't panning out. God had told me to shut it down. It was embarrassing, and I didn't know why He would do that to me. I had just gotten to the place where I was obedient without kicking and screaming. I verified in prayer that He really wanted me to shut it down and did as He said. I remember that whole afternoon being upset, but also being led to a podcast discussing prayer. The host of the podcast stated that if you leave prayer without clarity and instruction, you haven't prayed. Conviction hit my heart; I wasn't giving God all of the time He required from me. I realized that God had been saying wake up at 5:30am for over a month and I refused to do it. I told myself I was in a waiting season and there was no need. One day God got real straight up with me, so I got it together and started to do it.

Once I started to get up early, I had more than enough time to just sit in His presence and talk. He started speaking to me about so many things that had been unanswered. He made it clear why I couldn't do certain things and placed my focus on the right thing. Even getting this book done was a part of me listening intently. I never knew I would be teaching other people about purpose and love. I honestly thought it was something that everybody already knew how to do. I thought there are enough people talking about love. I soon realized it simply wasn't true. When you open your mouth, fast and wait for your answers you will know what to do.

We have to come to God fervently; your answers can be revealed swiftly but these things take time. You are learning new habits to develop a true genuine relationship with God and see what He has in store. The reason we have to learn and grow in love before purpose is because it keeps us focused on God. At times, God will give us instructions and we begin to do the work and then decide to go our own way instead of asking God how to accomplish the vision he gave us. We do this because we think one of two things: we either think we can't ask God for more help or we think that we don't need to ask Him for help. God has ordained your purpose, so you have to include Him with every detail of your purpose to prevent it from being perverted or taken over by your flesh or another outside source You have to walk into your calling in complete surrenderance to God so that you can truly be delivered and set free. On this journey to purpose, you will discover there are so many areas we haven't dealt with that need to be addressed. Recently God delivered me from unforgiveness and selfishness. This came after I really learned about love and it was exposed. It's so important that we allow God to use us. That can be one of the keys to your true destiny and identity.

After you do these consistently this is where it gets hard. With God, He tells you what to do and then you have to do it. We have to remember the God we serve. He will give you vision and provision, but you have to go generate the wealth. Yes, it's true, your purpose can be the key to you creating the wealth for generations to come. There is strategy directly from God that you have to work at. In Deuteronomy it states:

But remember the LORD your God, for it is he who gives you the ability to produce wealth, and so confirms his covenant, which he swore to your ancestors, as it is today.
Deuteronomy 8:18 NIV

The problem is, we know that God has given us the power and we create the plans, however where we fall short is when we do not implement or immediately go after what God tells us to do. Before I started to take my life in entrepreneurship seriously, I would get downloads and continue to put them off. I would also tell other people about it and watch them implement. I would watch them flourish and then I would get mad. I would displace my anger on them when really, I needed to place that on myself. I was the one not moving and doing what I was called to. Sometimes we forget that God's will is going to get done whether you move or not. God literally has been putting me on before time and I didn't listen. He told me to start a podcast before it was popular but guess who sat on it? Me. He also began telling me to speak about love sometime last year. Now I see this type of coaching being done more often than it was a couple years ago. See, I didn't understand why God was telling me to do stuff, so I didn't move. Now that I have grown in Christ, I understand I do not need to know why. I just need to move and trust him. Now that I love and trust Him, I can just move. Let me give you some inside scoop; I never thought I could teach about love and never knew I would write a book that details this much transparency; detailing parts of my walk with Christ. Now that I have a better understanding of God, I realize that although I have no idea where He is taking me, I am open and ready to go there.

For the Spirit God gave us does not make us timid, but gives us power, love and self-discipline.
2 Timothy 1:7 NIV

Another issue that could arise after discovering your purpose is fear; I too have dealt with this. Majority of my life, I have lived in fear, but of all of the fears I battled it was the fear of success. I think this fear was rooted in the things I have seen in my family and in life in general. I am someone who has entrepreneurs in my family. I have watched the highs and lows of being an entrepreneur, some became successful and then had to switch gears due to things in and out of their control. I have seen large companies get a lot of backlash. I have also watched people in ministry leading people down the wrong way. All these people are successful. I know that whatever God blows on will be great, so I was afraid that I wasn't ready. Afraid I didn't have capacity to handle what God has called me to be. Eventually I got tired of myself. I was tired of helping other people, getting business coaches that didn't know as much as I did. I was over it. I knew it was time for me to do it scared. God didn't give me the spirit of fear, so I know he was tricking me. He was using one of his fruits to knock me out so I would never start. Your enemy knows how God works; He knows that God will use someone else. I refuse to just let him win. So, I did it scared. I do everything scared I launched my nonprofit in FALL 2019 while being afraid of success but trusting that God will take care of everything. Although, my bank account said no, God said yes. We launched with a three-day retreat and left without owing anyone any money. Now in 2020, we have had other events and are on to more initiatives. This showed me, that if God be for me who can be against me. God has me and everything attached to my purpose in Hands.

In 2 Timothy 1:7, they describe that God gives us power, love and self-discipline. These are some fruits of the spirit. If we fill up with more of these and less of the things that are not like God, we will be more like Him. We will be bolder, stronger and more focused. We owe it to God to do what we are called to. You are out of line if you learn about God's love, find your purpose and then just sit on it. We have to move and overflow to build up the kingdom. As you move into purpose, you will start to get other fruits of the spirit.

But everyone who hears these words of mine and does not put them into practice is like a foolish man who built his house on sand. Matthew 7:26 NIV

To properly walk in your God given purpose your foundation is so important. When our foundation isn't correct, this is what you will do. There are so many things I tried and failed at because I didn't seek God's will. I was doing my own will. My will cannot stand because it's not a good foundation. I was being taken out in the first round. When I first shared my story in 2017, I spent a lot of time depressed because the way I wanted to do things wasn't generating income. I had a book, and that was it. No one was asking me to speak; I didn't even know how to get a speaking engagement. I couldn't afford to have books on hand. I didn't know how to make more money with one book. When I went back and started to speak to God, He began to reveal where I messed up. We get so excited sometimes that we forget that we have a flesh we are fighting and an enemy that hates us.

It's important that we don't miss the steps that God has for us. As you start to go through these steps and grow in love, it's important to stay sensitive to the spirit. We all are subject to falling because we are human. To think it can't happen to us is also us being foolish. I just knew that writing that first book was the only reason I was here on earth. I knew that I was supposed to write this one book and my life would just be great. I realized my foundation wasn't good, and I was a tree not bearing good fruit.

"Watch out for false prophets. They come to you in sheep's clothing, but inwardly they are ferocious wolves. 16 By their fruit you will recognize them. Do people pick grapes from thorn bushes, or figs from thistles? Likewise, every good tree bears good fruit, but a bad tree bears bad fruit. A good tree cannot bear bad fruit, and a bad tree cannot bear good fruit. Every tree that does not bear good fruit is cut down and thrown into the fire. Thus, by their fruit you will recognize them. Matthew 15-20. NIV

You can't bear good fruit if God didn't plant you. God will make sure your fruit is good if you let him. If you don't let Him, even after you find your purpose, you may miss something. Your purpose is much bigger than leaving your job, generating wealth, and feeding your family. It's meant to heal you, change you and grow you so you can help other people as well. I have quickly had so much growth. It started with me doing something I was extremely scared to do. I left a great paying job for several reasons but I thought the main one was so I could start a business and get off the clock. I soon realized that He wanted me, just me. I had work to do in the kingdom but before I could get to that work, I had to start with me. I had to get a solid foundation in God. This is what you have to do in order to bear good fruit. You have to make sure you are doing the things listed in this book and implementing what He said how He said it. It's God's job to tell you and it's your job do it.

"Let love and faithfulness never leave you; bind them around your neck, write them on the tablet of your heart. Then you will win favor and a good name in the sight of God and man." Proverbs 3:3-4 NIV

After we have done our part, implemented the things God has called us to we have to keep our perspective. When you move and operate in the greatest command which is love, attacks become even more real. We are responsible to not let that take us off guard. As we grow, God will send the people we are called to and they will look how we used to look. This will be the biggest thing that is irritating. You may even begin to forget what you used to look like, which is fine. You have to remember to keep love and faithfulness in your heart. Without it in your heart you may find yourself doing things against the rules of engagement God created for you. I want you to think about a scandal you heard in the kingdom. Do you think they were always scandalous? Probably not. At some point, they were called and did it God's way. At some point they got caught up in what God gave them. They may have started to fall into things like idolatry, hatred, selfishness, unforgiveness and/or perversion. I want you to understand and keep love in the forefront of your mind. Make sure you're write it on your heart so you can love God, yourself and others the right way.

Prayer: For Loving into Purpose

God, we love you and thank you for being a magnificent, and wonderful God
We bless your glorious name, You are the Great I am
We ask for Forgiveness of our sins
Forgive us for not moving and operating in love as you described
In 1 Corinthians 13
Forgive us for falling into the fruits of the world and not the fruits of the spirit
Forgive us for being disobedient to your word and your will
We thank you for the opportunity to come to you about everything
We thank you for answering all our prayers
We thank you for life, for peace, for love for joy
Lord, we thank you that we are chosen for your word says many are called few are chosen
Lord we come to you to submit to your will and lose our own will.
We ask that you give us supernatural understanding of our God Given Purpose
We ask that you show us how to go deeper with you
Lord we ask for strategy, we ask for vision and provision
In your word it says we have the power wealth
We know that our purpose is tied into our wealth generation
We ask that you deliver us from everything that seeks to stop us
Including unforgiveness, idolatry, fear, pain and deceit
We come against procrastination and stagnation and loss freedom and a sudden attitude
Your word says that you can come suddenly we ask that

your suddenly come swifter than we can imagine.
Lord we ask that you show us where we are failing
Plant us on solid grown the ground you set before us in your book
You are the potter and we are the clay.
We ask that you prepare us for where you are taking us in purpose.
Continue to download your vision and manifest the ideas you have given us.
Lord teach us how to discern spirits so that we know when it's you and when to rebuke a spirit off our purpose.
Lord we love you and we thank you now for everything you are doing,
We ask all these in Jesus name, Amen.

REFERENCES

-All scriptures are from the New International Version, English Standard Version, International Standard Version or King James Version as listed in the blue letter bible website. Next to each scripture the version is listed and can be found here: https://www.blueletterbible.org/

-**Footnote A:** Google Dictionary (2020) Retrieved From: https://www.google.com/search?sxsrf=ALeKk00Y5tSfBkJ KE2fkDTgxBF9emiQ3Yw:1599108369928&q=Dictionary& stick=H4sIAAAAAAAAAONQesSoyi3w8sc9YSmZSWtOXm MU4-LzL0jNc8lMLsnMz0ssqrRiUWJKzeNZxMqFEAMA7_ QXqzcAAAA&zx=1599108407733#dobs=patience

-**Footnote B:** Kindness (2019) Retrieved from: https://www.merriam-webster.com/dictionary/kindness

-**Footnote C:** Fruit of the Spirit: Kindness (2010) Retrieved from https://lifehopeandtruth.com/god/holy-spirit/the-fruit-of-the-spirit/fruit-of-the-spirit-kindness/).

-**Footnote D:** Footnote F: Merriam-Webster Dictionary (2019) Boast. Retrieved from: https://www.merriam-webster.com/thesaurus/boast

-Footnote E: Google Dictionary (2020). Pride. Retrieved from: https://www.google.com/search?sxsrf=ALeKk01Rw-LsbFKpU-HFForaWQGRqT_zhWA%3A1600126697038&source=hp&ei=-6f5fX5IEiMfmAriVhYgI&q=pride+definition&oq=pride+defin&gs_lcp=CgZwc3ktYWIQARgAMgoIABCxAxBGEPkBMgIIADICCAAyAggAMgIIADICCAAyAggAMgIIADICCAAyAggAOgQIIxAnOggILhDHARCjAjoLCC4QsQMQxwEQowI6BQgAELEDOgsILhCxAxCDARCTAjoCCC46CAgAELEDEIMBOggILhCxAxCDAToFCC4QsQM6CAguELEDEJMCUIoUWOArYNU9aABwAHgCgAHMAogBywuSAQc1LjQuMS4xmAEAoAEBqgEHZ3dzLXdpeg&sclient=psy-ab

-Footnote F: Merriam-Webster Dictionary (2019) Self-Seeking. Retrieved from: https://www.merriam-webster.com/thesaurus/self%20seeking

-Footnote G: Fort Gary Women's Resource Center (2018) Retrieved from: http://fgwrc.ca/wp-content/uploads/2018/10/Coping-and-Self-care.pdf

www.ingramcontent.com/pod-product-compliance
Lightning Source LLC
Chambersburg PA
CBHW070100100426
42743CB00012B/2615